THE
BULLDOG

by Charlotte Wilcox

Consultant:
Lee Schulz
St. Paul/Minneapolis Bulldog Club

CAPSTONE
HIGH/LOW BOOKS
an imprint of Capstone Press
Mankato, Minnesota

Capstone High/Low Books are published by Capstone Press
818 North Willow Street • Mankato, MN 56001
http://www.capstone-press.com

Library of Congress Cataloging-in-Publication Data
Wilcox, Charlotte.
    The bulldog/by Charlotte Wilcox.
        p. cm. — (Learning about dogs)
    Includes bibliographical references (p. 44) and index.
    Summary: Discusses the history, habits, and care of the bulldog, a former
fighting dog, which can now be a lovable pet.
    ISBN 0-7368-0004-2
    1. Bulldog—Juvenile literature. [1. Bulldog. 2. Dogs.] I. Title. II. Series:
Wilcox, Charlotte. Learning about dogs.
SF429.B85W55 1999
636.72—dc21
                                                                    98-18142
                                                                       CIP
                                                                        AC

Editorial Credits

Matt Doeden, editor; Timothy Halldin, cover designer; Sheri Gosewisch,
    photo researcher

Photo Credits

Faith A. Uridel, 17, 22
Kent & Donna Dannen, 10, 13, 18, 26, 36, 43
Mark Raycroft, 4, 9, 24, 29, 30, 38, 46
Matt Doeden, 34
Photo Network/Nancy Hoyt Belcher, cover
Reynolds Photography, 14
Unicorn/Christian Mundt, 6; Jim Hays, 33
Valan Photos/Ralph A. Reinhold, 21

Table of Contents

Quick Facts about the Bulldog

Description

Height: Bulldogs stand 12 to 14 inches (30 to 36 centimeters) tall. Height is measured from the ground to the withers. The withers are the tops of the shoulders.

Weight: Most bulldogs weigh from 40 to 50 pounds (18 to 23 kilograms).

Physical features: Bulldogs are short and wide. Their faces have lots of loose, wrinkled skin. They have flat noses, small ears, and short tails.

Colors: Bulldogs can be white, red, tan, brindle, or piebald. Brindle is streaked shades of a color. Piebald is white with patches of another color.

Development

Place of origin: Bulldogs came from England.

History of breed: Bulldogs came from large cattle dogs. People later bred them to fight bulls.

Numbers: United States dog clubs register about 12,000 bulldogs each year. Register means to record a dog's breeding record with an official club. Canadian dog clubs register about 500 bulldogs each year.

Uses

Most bulldogs in North America are family pets.

Chapter 1

A Fighting Past

People often think of bulldogs as fighters. People sometimes call rough or pushy people bulldogs. But these ideas about bulldogs are from the past. Bulldogs are no longer fighters.

Early bulldogs were good at fighting sports. People enjoyed watching bulldogs fight other animals such as bulls. But over time, people began to realize it was unkind to make animals fight. Today, it is against the law in most places to make animals fight.

People often think of bulldogs as fighters.

Modern Bulldogs

Modern bulldogs are lovable pets. They are calm and quiet. They get along well with people and other animals. They are not very active.

Some people do not understand how such calm dogs came from fighters. Years ago, many bulldogs were unsafe. Bulldogs were faithful to their masters. But they often attacked strangers or other animals. They were a danger to children.

Later, people kept only the friendly bulldogs as pets. People did not let dangerous bulldogs have puppies. Modern bulldogs came from the friendly bulldogs.

Other Bulldog Breeds

English bulldog is another name for a true bulldog. Other dog breeds have the name bulldog. But they are different from true bulldogs. These breeds include the American bulldog, the French bulldog, and the Olde English bulldog.

Dogs from these breeds are related to English bulldogs. These new breeds have different

French bulldogs are smaller than English bulldogs.

features than English bulldogs. American
bulldogs are larger than English bulldogs.
French bulldogs are smaller. Olde English
bulldogs are the most recent breed of bulldog.
People bred them to look more like bulldogs
from 200 years ago. People bred English
bulldogs with other dogs such as pit bull terriers
to produce Olde English bulldogs.

Chapter 2

The Beginnings of the Breed

Early bulldogs came from mastiffs. Mastiffs came to Europe from Asia thousands of years ago. Mastiffs are large and strong dogs. They have powerful jaws. Powerful jaws make mastiffs good fighters.

Mastiffs had many jobs during the Middle Ages (A.D. 500 to 1500). Many pulled carts or carried packs on their backs. Some mastiffs helped their owners hunt wild animals. Others guarded cattle and sheep from wolves. These mastiffs became the first bulldogs.

Early bulldogs came from mastiffs.

Bulldogs helped people who worked with large animals such as bulls. These people included farmers and butchers. Bulls were dangerous. Bulldogs protected their owners from bulls. The bulldogs would bite angry bulls.

Handling a Bull

Early bulldogs showed little fear of bulls. A bulldog would attack a bull that put the dog's owner in danger. A bulldog would jump up and use its teeth to grab a bull's nose or ear. The dog would hang on with its powerful jaws. This would get the bull's attention. It allowed the dog's owner to get the bull under control.

Early bulldogs were strong and brave. But many of them were too large to control bulls. Bulls could attack large dogs easily. Small, fast bulldogs could handle bulls more easily than large bulldogs could. Bulls could not easily use their horns to gore small dogs.

Bulldogs protected their owners from bulls for centuries. Many bulldogs gave up their lives

Small bulldogs could handle bulls more easily than large bulldogs could.

to save their owners. Bulls gored many bulldogs. Bulls stepped on many other bulldogs.

A New Sport
Good bulldogs were valuable to farmers and butchers. Dog breeders started having contests to show off their bulldogs. People watched the

contests to see which breeders had the best bulldogs.

To begin a contest, people chained a bull to a post. They commanded a bulldog to grab the bull's nose with its teeth. They recorded the length of time the bulldog could hold onto the bull. These contests became a sport known as bullbaiting. Bullbaiting was especially popular in England during the 1700s and 1800s.

Breeders developed rules for this new sport. Each bulldog had one minute to grab a bull's nose. Then the dog had to hang on for five minutes. After five minutes, the bulldog's owner forced the dog's mouth open. The owner often made the dog repeat the process. Dogs received points for catching a bull in one minute. They received more points if they held on for five minutes. The dog with the most points won the contest. Today, bullbaiting is illegal in most countries.

People bred bulldogs to have flat noses.

Changes in the Breed

People began breeding early bulldogs with dogs that had short, flat noses. Bulldogs with flat noses could breathe more easily while holding a bull's nose. This allowed them to hold on longer. Breeders also bred their dogs to have powerful jaws. This combination gave the bulldogs large, square heads. Breeders continued breeding bulldogs to have small bodies. Bulldogs with small bodies did not get hurt as easily.

Fewer farmers and butchers needed bulldogs during the 1600s and 1700s. Farmers bred cattle to be slower and heavier. Slow bulls were easier for people to control than quicker bulls. People still used bulldogs for bullbaiting. People also made bulldogs fight other animals such as bears. Bulldogs became more and more fierce through the years.

Bulldogs have large, square heads.

Chapter 3

The Development of the Breed

During the 1700s and 1800s, people bred bulldogs just for bullbaiting. Each of the dogs' features helped them fight. Even the bulldogs' wrinkled skin was perfect for bullbaiting. Wrinkled skin kept bulls' blood out of the dogs' eyes.

Over the years, bulldog breeders kept only the dogs with the largest heads. They also kept the dogs with small bodies and short legs. These features made bulldogs useless for farmwork. Bulldogs no longer could serve as herding dogs. They could only fight.

People bred bulldogs with small bodies and short legs.

No Longer Needed

The bulldog's fate changed forever during the 1800s. Many people of that time believed bullbaiting was wrong. People believed the sport caused unnecessary harm to both bulls and dogs.

The English government made bullbaiting illegal in 1835. Other dogfighting sports became illegal at about the same time. People no longer had any use for bulldogs. Many breeders stopped raising them. The bulldog breed almost disappeared.

Some people thought bulldogs were worth saving. These people believed bulldogs could become good pets. Owners began breeding more docile bulldogs. These bulldogs were calm and easy to manage.

Calm Bulldogs

Before 1835, people bought only the most fierce bulldogs. Fierce dogs won more fights than docile dogs. After 1835, people bred only

After 1835, owners bred docile bulldogs.

the friendliest bulldogs. The bulldogs these people bred grew increasingly docile over the years. They lost their fierce nature. The new, docile bulldogs lacked the energy of previous bulldogs. They no longer behaved like fighters.

These bulldogs became one of England's most popular pets. The bulldog was among the first breeds recognized by the Kennel Club of England. The Kennel Club of England began in 1873. This group keeps track of dog breeds in England.

People brought bulldogs to North America during the mid-1800s. The Bulldog Club of America began in 1890. This club helps people find and breed healthy bulldogs. It helped the bulldog become a popular pet across North America. Today, the American Kennel Club registers about 12,000 bulldogs each year. The Canadian Kennel Club registers about 500 each year.

Today's bulldogs lack the energy of previous bulldogs.

Chapter 4
The Bulldog Today

People call the look on bulldogs' faces a sourmug. This is because bulldogs' large mouths and loose skin often make them look angry. But bulldogs are not usually angry. They get along well with people. They are among the quietest and friendliest of dog breeds.

Appearance
Bulldogs are short and wide. They are 12 to 14 inches (30 to 36 centimeters) tall. Their height is measured from the ground to the withers. The withers are the tops of the shoulders. Female bulldogs weigh about 40 pounds (18 kilograms).

People call the look on bulldogs' faces a sourmug.

Males weigh about 50 pounds (23 kilograms).

Bulldogs have distinct features. Their faces have lots of loose, wrinkled skin. They have dark eyes and flat, black noses. Bulldogs have small, round ears. They have short tails. Their tails can be either straight or screwed. Screwed tails are curled. Bulldogs can be white, red, tan, brindle, or piebald. Brindle is streaked shades of a color. Piebald is white with patches of another color.

Health Problems

Bulldogs suffer from many health problems. Many of these problems occur because of the way people bred bulldogs years ago. Some of the features that once made bulldogs good fighters are harmful to their health today.

Bulldogs' short, flat noses cause breathing problems. Bulldogs sometimes gulp air into their stomachs. This causes them to burp and

Bulldogs' faces have lots of loose, wrinkled skin.

pass gas often. Bulldogs also snore loudly.
Many bulldogs drool.

Bulldogs cannot breathe sometimes when
given anesthetics. An anesthetic is a drug or gas
that makes patients sleep and blocks pain.
Veterinarians give anesthetics to animals before
operations. Bulldogs must receive special care
if they need operations.

Birth Problems
The shape of bulldogs' bodies causes birth
problems. Female bulldogs' rear ends are
small and narrow. Bulldog puppies have large
heads. The puppies' heads often become
stuck when females give birth. This puts both
puppies and mothers in danger.

Bulldog mothers often do not push hard
enough for their puppies to be born. Healthy
puppies can die before they are born.
Veterinarians perform operations to remove
the puppies.

Veterinarians may give bulldogs anesthetics

Bulldog puppies have large heads.

for these operations. Female bulldogs that
receive anesthetics may not know they have had
puppies. When they wake up, they do not
understand that the puppies are their own. They
may not feed them or care for them.

Chapter 5

Owning a Bulldog

Bulldogs are one of the most expensive dog breeds to buy. This is because so many puppies die at birth. It is also because bulldogs often need extra care.

Finding a new bulldog takes time. Dog shows are good places to start looking. This is where top breeders show their dogs. These breeders may be able to help people who want to buy bulldogs. Local bulldog clubs have names of good breeders.

Few good breeders sell bulldogs through pet stores. Most breeders warn people not to buy dogs at pet stores. These dogs often are unhealthy.

Bulldogs are one of the most expensive dog breeds to buy.

Caring for a Bulldog

Bulldogs do not require as much attention as some dog breeds. Bulldogs do not need much exercise. One walk per day is usually enough. Bulldog owners do not need to groom their dogs much because of the bulldog's short fur. Bulldogs must be brushed once per week. Owners should bathe bulldogs only when needed.

Bulldogs cannot stand much heat. They must cool themselves off by panting. Panting is hard and fast breathing. Bulldogs' throats can swell if they become too hot. This can kill them.

Many owners keep their bulldogs in air-conditioned homes. Others provide fans or extra shade for their bulldogs. Some owners give their bulldogs small swimming pools. Bulldogs can lie in the water to keep cool. But bulldogs should never go into deep water. They cannot swim.

Bulldogs pant when they are hot.

A bulldog may eat about one pound (.5 kilograms) of dry dog food each day.

Finding a Lost Dog

Owners should be sure their dogs have identification. Some owners attach tags with a name and address to their dogs' collars. Others give their dogs tattoos. Tattoos are marks on the skin. Tattoos can have information about how to contact a dog's owner.

Some people have veterinarians place microchips under their dogs' skin. Veterinarians can scan these tiny chips in lost dogs. The microchips contain information about the dog and how to contact its owner.

Feeding a Bulldog

Pet stores carry several forms of dog food. The most common forms are dry, semimoist, and canned. Bulldogs can eat any one of these forms. Some bulldog owners add a spoonful of vegetable oil to their dogs' food. Vegetable oil helps keep bulldogs' fur healthy.

Owners should not let their bulldogs eat too much. Bulldogs gain weight easily. A bulldog may eat about one pound (.5 kilograms) of dry or semimoist food each day. It may eat two or three cans of canned food per day instead.

Bulldogs need plenty of water. Owners should make sure their dogs can drink as often as they want. This should be at least three times per day.

It is best not to bother a bulldog while it eats. Bulldogs may be protective of their food.

The Bulldog's Future

Bulldogs are no longer fighting dogs. They are quiet and friendly. They are one of the most popular dog breeds in the world.

Bulldogs still have health problems as a result of their breeding. But breeders and veterinarians are working to change this. They are trying to breed only the healthiest bulldogs.

Bulldogs should drink at least three times per day.

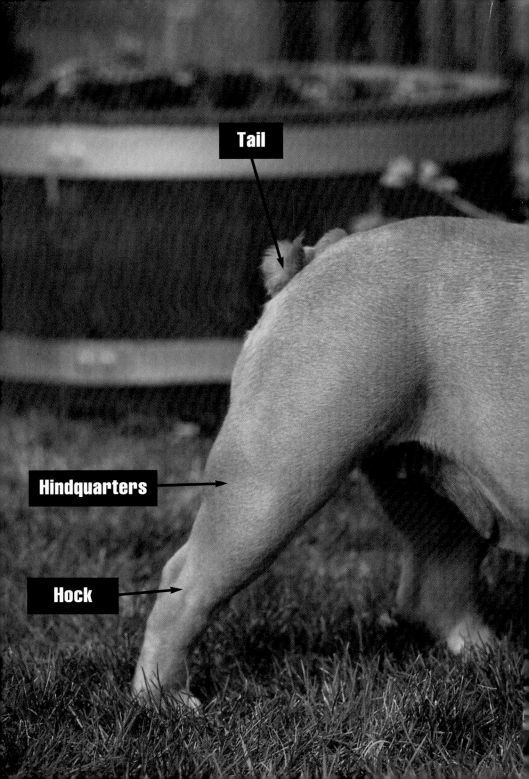

Quick Facts about Dogs

Dog Terms

A male dog is called a dog. A female dog is called a bitch. A young dog is a puppy until it is one year old. A newborn puppy is a whelp until it no longer depends on its mother's milk. A family of puppies born at one time is called a litter.

Life History

Origin: All dogs, wolves, coyotes, and dingoes descended from a single wolflike species. Dogs have been friends of people since early times.

Types: There are about 350 different dog breeds. Dogs come in different sizes and colors. Adult dogs weigh from two to 200 pounds (one to 91 kilograms). They stand from six to 36 inches (15 to 91 centimeters) tall.

Reproduction: Dogs mature at six to 18 months. Puppies are born two months after breeding. An average litter is three to six puppies, but litters of 15 or more are possible.

Development: Newborn puppies cannot see or hear. Their ears and eyes open one to two weeks after birth. They try to walk about two weeks after birth. Their teeth begin to come in about three weeks after birth.

Life span: Dogs are fully grown at two years. They may live up to 15 years.

The Dog's Super Senses

Smell: Dogs have a strong sense of smell. Dogs use their noses even more than their eyes and ears. They recognize people, animals, and objects just by smelling them. They may recognize smells from long distances. They also may remember smells for long periods of time.

Hearing: Dogs hear better than people do. Dogs can hear noises from long distances. They also hear high-pitched sounds that people cannot hear.

Sight: Dogs' eyes are on the sides of their heads. They can see twice as wide around their heads as people can. Some scientists believe dogs cannot see colors.

Touch: Dogs enjoy being petted more than almost any other animal. They also can feel vibrations from approaching trains or the earliest stages of earthquakes.

Taste: Dogs cannot taste much. This is partly because their sense of smell is so strong that it overpowers their taste.

Navigation: Dogs often can find their way through crowded streets or across miles of wilderness without any guidance. This is a special ability that scientists do not fully understand.

Words to Know

anesthetic (an-iss-THET-ik)—a drug or gas that makes patients sleep and blocks pain

brindle (BRIN-duhl)—streaked shades of a color

bullbaiting (BUL-bayt-ing)—a sport in which a bulldog bites and holds a bull's nose

docile (DOSS-uhl)—calm and easy to manage

gore (GOR)—to pierce with horns

groom (GROOM)—to brush and clean an animal

litter (LIT-ur)—a family of puppies born to one mother at one time

panting (PANT-ing)—hard and fast breathing

piebald (PYE-bawld)—white with patches of another color

register (REJ-uh-stur)—to record a dog's breeding records with an official club

sourmug (SOUR-muhg)—the angry look on a bulldog's face

veterinarian (vet-ur-uh-NER-ee-uhn)—a person trained to treat the sicknesses and injuries of animals

withers (WITH-urs)—the tops of an animal's shoulders

To Learn More

Driscoll, Laura. *All about Dogs and Puppies.* All Aboard Books. New York: Grosset & Dunlap, 1998.

Hansen, Ann Larkin. *Dogs.* Popular Pet Care. Minneapolis: Abdo & Daughters, 1997.

Rosen, Michael J. *Kids' Best Field Guide to Neighborhood Dogs.* New York: Workman, 1993.

You can read articles about bulldogs in magazines such as *AKC Gazette, Dog Fancy, Dogs in Canada, Dog World,* and *Sourmug.*

Useful Addresses

American Kennel Club
5580 Centerview Drive
Raleigh, NC 27606

Bulldog Club of America
P.O. Box 248
Nobleton, FL 34661

Canadian Kennel Club
89 Skyway Avenue, Suite 100
Etobicoke, ON M9W 6R4
Canada

Confederation Bulldog Club
100-75 Burrows Hall Boulevard
Scarborough, ON M1B 1M7
Canada

Internet Sites

The American Kennel Club
http://www.akc.org

The Bulldog Club of America
http://www.thebca.org

Bulldog.org
http://bulldog.org

Regince Kennels
http://members.aol.com/regince/index.htm

Index